To my Wonderful Great-Grandchild:

_____

YOU ARE *Loved* MORE THAN YOU KNOW

You and Me

Dear Great-Grandchild   Date:_____

_____

_____

_____

_____

_____

_____

_____

_____

_____

_____

_____

_____

Dream Big
Little One...

Dear Great-Grandchild Date:_____

_____

_____

_____

_____

_____

_____

_____

_____

_____

_____

_____

_____

_____

_____

_____

_____

_____

Dream Big
Little One...

Dear Great-Grandchild   Date:_____

_____

_____

_____

_____

_____

_____

_____

_____

_____

_____

_____

_____

_____

Dream Big
Little One...

For Photos or Keepsakes:

Dear Great-Grandchild   Date:_____

_____
_____
_____
_____
_____
_____
_____
_____
_____
_____
_____
_____
_____

Dream Big
Little One...

Dear Great-Grandchild Date:_____

_____

_____

_____

_____

_____

_____

_____

_____

_____

_____

_____

_____

_____

Dream Big
Little One...

Dear Great-Grandchild   Date:_____

_____

_____

_____

_____

_____

_____

_____

_____

_____

_____

_____

_____

_____

_____

_____

Dream Big
Little One...

For Photos or Keepsakes:

Dear Great-Grandchild   Date:_____

_____
_____
_____
_____
_____
_____
_____
_____
_____
_____
_____
_____
_____
_____
_____
_____

Dream Big
Little One...

Dear Great-Grandchild   Date:_____

_____

_____

_____

_____

_____

_____

_____

_____

_____

_____

_____

_____

Dream Big
Little One...

Dear Great-Grandchild   Date:_____

_____

_____

_____

_____

_____

_____

_____

_____

_____

_____

_____

_____

_____

_____

_____

Dream Big
Little One...

For Photos or Keepsakes:

Dear Great-Grandchild   Date:_____

_____

_____

_____

_____

_____

_____

_____

_____

_____

_____

_____

_____

_____

_____

_____

_____

_____

_____

Dream Big
Little One...

Dear Great-Grandchild   Date:_____

_____

_____

_____

_____

_____

_____

_____

_____

_____

_____

_____

_____

_____

Dream Big
Little One...

Dear Great-Grandchild   Date:_____

_____

_____

_____

_____

_____

_____

_____

_____

_____

_____

_____

_____

_____

_____

_____

_____

Dream Big
Little One...

For Photos or Keepsakes:

Dear Great-Grandchild   Date:_____

_____

_____

_____

_____

_____

_____

_____

_____

_____

_____

_____

_____

_____

_____

_____

_____

_____

Dream Big
Little One...

Dear Great-Grandchild   Date:_____

_____

_____

_____

_____

_____

_____

_____

_____

_____

_____

_____

_____

_____

_____

Dream Big
Little One...

Dear Great-Grandchild   Date:_____

_____

_____

_____

_____

_____

_____

_____

_____

_____

_____

_____

_____

_____

_____

_____

Dream Big
Little One...

For Photos or Keepsakes:

Dear Great-Grandchild   Date:_____

_____

_____

_____

_____

_____

_____

_____

_____

_____

_____

_____

_____

_____

_____

Dream Big
Little One...

Dear Great-Grandchild   Date:_____

_____

_____

_____

_____

_____

_____

_____

_____

_____

_____

_____

Dream Big
Little One...

Dear Great-Grandchild Date:_____

_____

_____

_____

_____

_____

_____

_____

_____

_____

_____

_____

_____

_____

_____

_____

_____

Dream Big
Little One...

For Photos or Keepsakes:

Dear Great-Grandchild   Date:_____

_____

_____

_____

_____

_____

_____

_____

_____

_____

_____

_____

_____

_____

Dream Big
Little One...

Dear Great-Grandchild   Date:_____

_____

_____

_____

_____

_____

_____

_____

_____

_____

_____

_____

_____

_____

Dream Big
Little One...

Dear Great-Grandchild Date:_____

_____
_____
_____
_____
_____
_____
_____
_____
_____
_____
_____
_____
_____
_____
_____

Dream Big
Little One...

For Photos or Keepsakes:

Dear Great-Grandchild   Date:_____

_____

_____

_____

_____

_____

_____

_____

_____

_____

_____

_____

_____

_____

_____

_____

_____

_____

Dream Big
Little One...

Dear Great-Grandchild   Date:_____

_____

_____

_____

_____

_____

_____

_____

_____

_____

_____

_____

_____

Dream Big
Little One...

Dear Great-Grandchild   Date:_____

_____

_____

_____

_____

_____

_____

_____

_____

_____

_____

_____

Dream Big
Little One...

For Photos or Keepsakes:

Dear Great-Grandchild Date:_____

_____

_____

_____

_____

_____

_____

_____

_____

_____

_____

_____

_____

_____

_____

_____

_____

_____

_____

Dream Big
Little One...

Dear Great-Grandchild   Date:_____

Dream Big
Little One...

Dear Great-Grandchild   Date:_____

_____

_____

_____

_____

_____

_____

_____

_____

_____

_____

_____

_____

_____

_____

_____

_____

_____

_____

_____

_____

_____

Dream Big
Little One...

For Photos or Keepsakes:

Dear Great-Grandchild   Date:_____

_____

_____

_____

_____

_____

_____

_____

_____

_____

_____

_____

_____

_____

_____

_____

_____

_____

_____

Dream Big
Little One...

Dear Great-Grandchild   Date:_____

_____

_____

_____

_____

_____

_____

_____

_____

_____

_____

_____

_____

Dream Big
Little One...

Dear Great-Grandchild   Date:_____

_____

_____

_____

_____

_____

_____

_____

_____

_____

_____

_____

_____

_____

_____

_____

_____

_____

Dream Big
Little One...

For Photos or Keepsakes:

Dear Great-Grandchild Date:_____

_____

_____

_____

_____

_____

_____

_____

_____

_____

_____

_____

_____

_____

Dream Big
Little One...

Dear Great-Grandchild   Date:_____

_____

_____

_____

_____

_____

_____

_____

_____

_____

_____

_____

_____

_____

Dream Big
Little One...

Dear Great-Grandchild Date:_____

Dream Big
Little One...

For Photos or Keepsakes:

Dear Great-Grandchild   Date:_____

_____

_____

_____

_____

_____

_____

_____

_____

_____

_____

_____

_____

_____

_____

Dream Big
Little One...

Dear Great-Grandchild Date:_____

_____

_____

_____

_____

_____

_____

_____

_____

_____

_____

_____

_____

_____

_____

_____

Dream Big
Little One...

Dear Great-Grandchild   Date:_____

_____

_____

_____

_____

_____

_____

_____

_____

_____

_____

_____

_____

_____

_____

_____

_____

_____

Dream Big
Little One...

For Photos or Keepsakes:

Dear Great-Grandchild   Date:_____

_____

_____

_____

_____

_____

_____

_____

_____

_____

_____

_____

_____

_____

_____

Dream Big
Little One...

Dear Great-Grandchild   Date:_____

_____

_____

_____

_____

_____

_____

_____

_____

_____

_____

_____

_____

_____

_____

_____

_____

Dream Big
Little One...

Dear Great-Grandchild   Date:_____

_____

_____

_____

_____

_____

_____

_____

_____

_____

_____

_____

_____

_____

_____

_____

_____

_____

Dream Big
Little One...

For Photos or Keepsakes:

Dear Great-Grandchild   Date:_____

_____

_____

_____

_____

_____

_____

_____

_____

_____

_____

_____

_____

_____

_____

_____

_____

_____

_____

Dream Big
Little One...

Dear Great-Grandchild   Date:_____

_____

_____

_____

_____

_____

_____

_____

_____

_____

_____

_____

_____

_____

Dream Big
Little One...

Dear Great-Grandchild   Date:_____

_____

_____

_____

_____

_____

_____

_____

_____

_____

_____

_____

_____

_____

_____

_____

Dream Big
Little One...

For Photos or Keepsakes:

Dear Great-Grandchild   Date:_____

_____

_____

_____

_____

_____

_____

_____

_____

_____

_____

_____

_____

_____

_____

_____

Dream Big
Little One...

Dear Great-Grandchild   Date:_____

_____

_____

_____

_____

_____

_____

_____

_____

_____

_____

_____

_____

Dream Big
Little One...

Dear Great-Grandchild   Date:_____

_____

_____
_____

_____
_____

_____
_____

_____
_____

_____
_____

_____
_____

_____
_____

_____
_____

_____
_____

_____

Dream Big
Little One...

For Photos or Keepsakes:

Dear Great-Grandchild   Date:_____

_____

_____

_____

_____

_____

_____

_____

_____

_____

_____

_____

_____

_____

_____

_____

Dream Big
Little One...

Dear Great-Grandchild   Date:_____

_____

_____

_____

_____

_____

_____

_____

_____

_____

_____

_____

_____

_____

Dream Big
Little One....

Dear Great-Grandchild   Date:_____

_____

_____

_____

_____

_____

_____

_____

_____

_____

_____

_____

_____

_____

Dream Big
Little One...

For Photos or Keepsakes:

Dear Great-Grandchild   Date:_____

_____

_____

_____

_____

_____

_____

_____

_____

_____

_____

_____

_____

Dream Big
Little One...

Dear Great-Grandchild Date:_____

_____

_____

_____

_____

_____

_____

_____

_____

_____

_____

_____

_____

_____

Dream Big
Little One...

Dear Great-Grandchild   Date:_____

_____
_____
_____
_____
_____
_____
_____
_____
_____
_____
_____
_____
_____
_____
_____
_____
_____
_____
_____
_____

Dream Big
Little One...

For Photos or Keepsakes:

Dear Great-Grandchild   Date:_____

_____

_____

_____

_____

_____

_____

_____

_____

_____

_____

_____

_____

_____

_____

_____

_____

Dream Big
Little One...

Dear Great-Grandchild   Date:_____

_____

_____

_____

_____

_____

_____

_____

_____

_____

_____

_____

_____

Dream Big
Little One...

Dear Great-Grandchild   Date:_____

_____

_____

_____

_____

_____

_____

_____

_____

_____

_____

_____

_____

_____

_____

_____

_____

_____

Dream Big
Little One...

For Photos or Keepsakes:

Dear Great-Grandchild   Date:_____

_____

_____

_____

_____

_____

_____

_____

_____

_____

_____

_____

_____

_____

_____

_____

_____

_____

Dream Big
Little One...

Dear Great-Grandchild   Date:_____

_____

_____

_____

_____

_____

_____

_____

_____

_____

_____

_____

Dream Big
Little One...

Dear Great-Grandchild   Date:_____

_____
_____
_____
_____
_____
_____
_____
_____
_____
_____
_____
_____
_____
_____
_____
_____
_____
_____
_____

Dream Big
Little One...

For Photos or Keepsakes:

Dear Great-Grandchild   Date:_____

_____
_____
_____
_____
_____
_____
_____
_____
_____
_____
_____
_____
_____
_____

Dream Big
Little One...

Dear Great-Grandchild Date:_____

_____

_____

_____

_____

_____

_____

_____

_____

_____

_____

_____

_____

_____

_____

Dream Big
Little One...

Dear Great-Grandchild Date:_____

_____

_____

_____

_____

_____

_____

_____

_____

_____

_____

_____

_____

_____

_____

_____

_____

_____

Dream Big
Little One...

For Photos or Keepsakes:

Dear Great-Grandchild   Date:_____

_____

_____

_____

_____

_____

_____

_____

_____

_____

_____

_____

_____

_____

_____

_____

_____

_____

_____

_____

_____

_____

_____

_____

Dream Big
Little One...

Dear Great-Grandchild   Date:_____

_____

_____

_____

_____

_____

_____

_____

_____

_____

_____

_____

_____

Dream Big
Little One...

Dear Great-Grandchild Date:_____

_____

_____

_____

_____

_____

_____

_____

_____

_____

_____

_____

_____

_____

Dream Big
Little One...

For Photos or Keepsakes:

Dear Great-Grandchild   Date:_____

_____

_____

_____

_____

_____

_____

_____

_____

_____

_____

_____

_____

_____

Dream Big
Little One...

Dear Great-Grandchild   Date:_____

_____

_____

_____

_____

_____

_____

_____

_____

_____

_____

_____

_____

_____

Dream Big
Little One...

Dear Great-Grandchild   Date:_____

_____

_____

_____

_____

_____

_____

_____

_____

_____

_____

_____

_____

_____

_____

_____

_____

Dream Big
Little One...

For Photos or Keepsakes:

Dear Great-Grandchild Date:_____

_____

_____

_____

_____

_____

_____

_____

_____

_____

_____

_____

_____

_____

Dream Big
Little One...

Dear Great-Grandchild   Date:_____

_____

_____

_____

_____

_____

_____

_____

_____

_____

_____

_____

_____

_____

Dream Big
Little One...

Dear Great-Grandchild   Date:_____

Dream Big
Little One...

For Photos or Keepsakes:

Dear Great-Grandchild Date:_____

Dream Big
Little One...

Dear Great-Grandchild   Date:_____

_____

_____

_____

_____

_____

_____

_____

_____

_____

_____

_____

_____

Dream Big
Little One...

Dear Great-Grandchild Date:_____

_____
_____
_____
_____
_____
_____
_____
_____
_____
_____
_____
_____
_____
_____
_____
_____
_____
_____

Dream Big
Little One...

For Photos or Keepsakes:

Dear Great-Grandchild Date:_____

_____

_____

_____

_____

_____

_____

_____

_____

_____

_____

_____

_____

_____

_____

_____

_____

Dream Big
Little One...

Dear Great-Grandchild   Date:_____

_____

_____

_____

_____

_____

_____

_____

_____

_____

_____

_____

Dream Big
Little One...

Dear Great-Grandchild   Date:_____

_____

_____

_____

_____

_____

_____

_____

_____

_____

_____

_____

_____

_____

_____

_____

_____

_____

Dream Big
Little One...

For Photos or Keepsakes:

KEEPING IT

WHAT'S MOST IMPORTANT TO ME:

WHAT I'M MOST GRATEFUL FOR:

DATES TO *Remember*
Me — *You*

YOU ARE MY
Everything

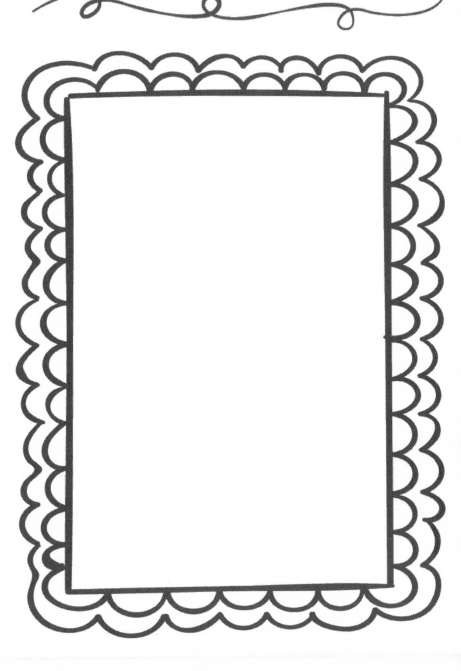